Dorothy Dunnett Society and
Historical Writers' Association

Short Story Competition 2024

Published by the Dorothy Dunnett Society, Edinburgh, and the Historical Writers' Association, London.

The Dorothy Dunnett Society is a Scottish Charitable Incorporated Organization No. SC030649.
The Historical Writers' Assocation is registered in England, number 09132674 at
The Union Building, 51-59 Rose Lane, Norwich NR 1 1BY.

Selection and interviews copyright c Dorothy Dunnett Society/Historical Writers' Association 2024
Copyright of individual stories rests with the authors

Photographs c the individual photographers

First published by the Dorothy Dunnett Society/ Historical Writers' Association in 2024

The authors have asserted their rights under the Copyright, Designs and Patents Act 1988 to be identified as the authors of this work.

All rights reserved. Apart from any fair dealing for the purpose of private study, research, criticism or review, as permitted under the Copyright, Designs and Patents Act 1988, no part of this publication may be reproduced, stored in a retrieval system, or transmitted in any form or by any means, electronic, mechanical, photocopying, recording or otherwise, without the prior written permission of the copyright owner.

Dorothy Dunnett Society and
Historical Writers' Association

Short Story Competition 2024

History is all very well but it's just the showcase. It is the arena in which your characters will perform, and which supplies the conflicts, stresses, dilemmas and the struggles they'll get through.
Dorothy Dunnett

Introduction..6

The Winning Story
St Kilda Bird Song by K F MacCarthy.........................9

Highly Commended
After Jutland, 1916 by Liz Kershaw...................................22

No Competition by Elaine O'Connor................................35

Shortlisted
Mother's Fury by Laura Karim..49

Bonfire Night by Muiread O'Hanlon....................................62

Nebraska by Cath Staincliffe..73

Short Story Competition 2024 Judges and Longlisted Authors..81

About the Dorothy Dunnett Society...............................83

About the Historical Writers' Association.......................85

INTRODUCTION

2024 was a bumper year for the Dorothy Dunnett Society and the Historical Writers' Association's Unpublished Short Story Competition. We received over two hundred entries covering every epoch of human history and were again delighted and humbled by the quality of the writing as well as very glad to have reached a new cohort of writers who are taking inspiration from the past. Creating a convincing world and telling a complete story with interesting, complex characters within the 3500 word limit is tough; writing a story that engages the reader emotionally and intellectually is even harder and our long and shortlisted writers achieved that, and managed deliver something fresh and satisfying too. Some stories were epic in their scope, others kept their focus tightly on a private moment, but all were remarkable exercises of empathy and imagination that created something magical on the page. Not only did their stories bring the past to life, they made it immediate, intimate, dramatic - they made it new.

All entries are judged anonymously, and we would like to thank our first readers for working through this years entries with such care and for helping us to put together such a strong longlist - it could have been twice as long. All the writers who reached that stage of the competition are working to a high standard and I do hope we shall hear from them again.

I thoroughly enjoyed listening to our final round

judges discussing and debating the longlist, sharing their thoughts on such a range of stories to pick the final six. We are very grateful to them for the time and trouble they took to consider the stories so thoughtfully. Once again, I think we've been entrusted with some real gems - from quiet moments of private struggle and sacrifice, or small but life changing triumphs, to moments that changed history, or might define an age. Time travel with us, and see how in the hands of great writers we can experience another time.

Our winner this year, *St Kilda Bird Song* by K.F. MacCarthy is a magical and immersive story of a late nineteenth century teacher on the remote island, told from diverse perspectives with fluency and confidence. It's both ambitious artistically and deeply moving, both poetic and grounded. A very special piece of writing about a remarkable place.

After Jutland, 1916 by Liz Kershaw, one of our highly commended stories is touching and assured. The story of motherhood and family is a portrait of a widow struggling to raise her three boys after losing her husband, and is all the more powerful thanks to the clean, character focussed writing. The use of the present tense makes it feel immediate and intimate producing a tale of ordinary heroism done with a light touch. Our second highly commended entry, *No Competition* by Elaine O'Connor is a gentle tale of triumph, full of quiet pride, but establishes its own particular voice from the first, wonderfully memorable line. A teacher fights to give a student her moment and changes her life.

Mother's Fury by Laura Karim is taught slice of violence and revenge at the climax of the peasant's revolt in 14th century England, thrillingly told. *Bonfire Night* by Muiread O'Hanlon offers a fresh and convincing voice of boyhood adventure in Ireland and *Nebraska* by Cath Staincliffe give us a richly-imagined story of frontier adventure and resilience.

We are proud and delighted to share these stories and writers with you.

WINNER
K.F. MacCarthy

About the Author

K.F. MacCarthy is a writer from South Yorkshire. She has been shortlisted for the Bournemouth Short Story Prize and the Alpine Fellowship's Academic Writing Prize, and was longlisted for the Historical Writers Association's Dorothy Dunnett Short Story Prize in 2022. She has a degree in History and French from the University of Oxford, where she gravitated towards Early Modern art and culture. Having specialised in sixteenth-century France, she then made life much more difficult than it needed to be by deciding to write a book set in late-fifteenth-century Florence.

Her fiction is grounded in cutting-edge academic research and aims to bring hidden aspects of history to vibrant life. She has attended Curtis Brown Creative's 'Writing Historical Fiction' course and Imogen Hermes Gowar's wonderful 'Writing the Past'. Her debut novel-in-progress tells the untold, interwoven stories of marginalised women in Quattrocento Florence. It won the Farnham Literary Festival's 'First Five Thousand' prize 2024 and was longlisted for the Cheshire Novel Prize 2024. She's researching a second novel set in a similar time and place, which uncovers another little-known story from the High Renaissance.

Her favourite writers of historical fiction are Sarah Dunant, Hilary Mantel and A.K. Blakemore. As someone fascinated by the Renaissance period in Europe, she is looking forward to exploring Dorothy Dunnett's fictional world and is planning to start with 'The House of Niccolò' series.

Find her on Instagram at @k.f.maccarthy

ST KILDA BIRD SONG
by K.F. MacCarthy

Unfurl a map of the world. Take your finger and place it on Scotland. Find Edinburgh. Then push up and west to Skye, then west again. Feel the paper hiss under the pad of your fingertip and keep going. Keep going and going for almost a hundred miles, your finger cutting through violent Atlantic waves, casting a looming shadow over the heads of minke whales. Stop. Can you see it? That speck. That pinprick-sized mote by the ridge in your fingernail.

The archipelago of St Kilda.

One swift origami fold of the map and you're a seabird, up high in the firmament above a churning navy sea. You hang in a vast blue dome, faintly divided by a bleeding line on the far horizon. Blue, blue, blue. It's all your beady eye is filled with. Tilt your wings and swoop down with the other shrieking fulmars and bonxies, towards columns of sheer, slick rock slicing out of the waves.

Descend closer still. The largest island, Hirta, is a shallow bowl tipped over to let in the sea at a sandy bay. There are no trees–there is no word for tree, here–only close-cropped grass and venerable sheep. Behind the bay, against all logic: a row of squat houses.

Dive down and spin through the air. You don't want to be a fulmar here. You'll end up salted in a barrel. They'll make a nail of your beak, an espadrille of your neck, a bottle of your stomach. They'll use the oil in your belly to light their lamps.

You could instead be a cleit. A boulder. A grassy hollow. You could be anything at all. This is a place where a cove has a memory, where a stream hears what you tell it. There is a soul in every thing.

Your wings corkscrew like a twirling magician's cloak and in a puff of feathers, you're a common moth, buffeted by the smack of a strong gust. Down a chimney you go and into a cave-dim room, singeing your wingtips on the fire before tumbling to the ground. Warmth. Loud chatter, some singing. Several pairs of bare children's feet miss you by inches. You've arrived in the midst of a gathering. You flit towards a window, cling to a curtain fold. Here, so far from humanity you might as well be on the surface of the moon, are the most unlikely of things. People.

There are 77 of them. There used to be more.

***

15th September, 1884

My dear friend,

It's past midnight, and light and paper are scarce, but I find it comforts me to write. To remember there is a world beyond the horizon.

I imagine you in your cosy office with the leather armchair by the fire. You must imagine me sitting on a rickety chair at a low table, with the rain lashing outside and the wind playing through the lintel like a reed instrument. I'm not yet used to the nights here. I wonder whether any islanders are awake to see the lamp flickering in my window. It's a beacon advertising my wakefulness. Worse, it's a profligate waste of fuel.

Three months into life as the first dedicated schoolmaster on St Kilda. I hardly know where to begin. I'm holding up well. You know me as a man of daring and resilience,

I think (I hope), and I am certainly putting those qualities to good use here. I have had several near-death experiences already. In fact, over summer I averaged about one per week. I've been taking part in the ceaseless, herculean effort required to survive here. Snaring fulmars and puffins, dangling off cliffs attached to a rope. Catching sheep. Fishing in some pretty lively seas. And of course teaching every weekday forenoon, which is what I was put here to do.

My students are making excellent progress. There are ten of them, ranged in age from five to eighteen. I've been tasked with teaching English, although I can converse perfectly well with them in Gaelic and they've also taught me a few Norse words. The brightest among them is a young man named Alexander Ferguson. I intend to leave my books behind for him when I go.

I've been welcomed warmly, in the main. The people are stout, generous and instinctively kind. There is one fly in my ointment. The Reverend John Mackay. All other hardships are bearable but I'm finding him a challenge, shall we say. The old man has been here some twenty years and is master of his own little dominion, as engrained in this community as the guano on the cliffs. I suppose the remoteness of location attracts a certain kind of character. Where I sought adventure, he sought something else. But enough on that. I'm dyspeptic after my supper of preserved eggs and to think on him further will make me bilious.

A note on the food. Everything here comes with a side of seabird. I witnessed the great annual massacre of fulmars in August. They were piled up higher than a house and the place was swirling with feathers. Every part of the bird is put to use but the oil is most revered. The islanders evangelise about the healing properties of this sticky, foul-smelling stuff. Worst of all, they add great spoonfuls of it to porridge and declare this oleaginous substance the finest breakfast in all Christendom. I am frequently hungry.

My lamp peters out. I shall tuck this letter into the pile along with all the others I can't send. No hope of a boat until April.

> *Your devoted friend,*
> *Dr Kenneth Campbell.*

***

You are a wooden cradle. Smooth with the feet and hands that have rocked you, carrying along your spine the imprint of the tiny souls you've held. The air in the shadowy room is close. Peat, smoke, blood. A woman struggles in the narrow space between life and death. You see the rounded rump of the crouching knee woman, the bramach-innilt. You see feverish cheeks, a dark tendril of hair plastered to a pale forehead. The struggle is long. Sunset. Sunrise. At its end is a gargled cry, repeating the refrain of the gulls outside. 'I'm alive, I'm alive, I'm alive.' The sway of dun tweed skirts over compacted earth. The knee woman takes a bird-stomach bottle from a shelf, turns it in her hand. She keeps her secrets close, bars all others from the room, but you see her do this. She anoints the cord with fulmar oil. Later, the delight of a bairn's spine along your spine again. Lachlan, mo chridhe, says the woman who gazes down. Lachlan, my heart. Chubby fists escaping their swaddling, sharp-nailed fingers playing at your sides. An absentminded toe on your rocker, the swish-swish and the fire crackling.

***

My dear friend,

I have noticed lately a division between the village and the manse, where the Reverend lives with his elderly sister and his housekeeper Ann MacDonald. Whenever I go to the manse for dinner, there is always some gossip offered at the table. I never comment, preferring to keep well out of such matters. But you can imagine how it is, in such a small place. Everything seems to close in and strife is intensified. The lady Ann MacDonald has quite the sharp tongue and she relishes cutting those she dislikes to ribbons with it. Likewise, Mackay favours certain islanders and castigates others. He says that though his influence has caused 'a change for the better as to their moral character', there remain pockets where Satan rules. What nonsense.

I thank God every day that I am able to converse fluently with the people in their own language. They have the truth directly from my mouth, and I the truth from them, and like this we understand each other. I'd rather spend my time in the village and take my meals among the families there. A third of the population left for Australia thirty years ago and those they left behind often ask me to write letters. They dictate them to me around the fire. It's a pleasant way to spend an evening.

***

You are the font in the new church, absorbing the cold. Close by, the Reverend is spouting his booming invective. Infecting the air. His leaden words press the people down into their pews, pool in the hollow of your basin. 'And the angels shall CAST them into a FURNACE of FIRE.' A fleck of spittle flies, lands in his grey whiskers. 'There shall be WAILING and GNASHING OF TEETH.' How silent it is, when he isn't here. How peaceful. Mrs Gillies, dowager, suppresses her sneeze in a handkerchief. The chill seeps from a pinewood pew into the meagre fat around Euphemia's hips until they are numb. The Reverend, a billy goat armed with the word of God, stamps his foot. The shockwave passes through your pedestal. Irritating.

***

There is a terrible plague of infant deaths here. I was speaking with Mackay about the lack of young children. He said that when babies come to the age of seven or eight days, 'they generally die'. Generally. As though it is accepted and unstoppable. They're afflicted with lockjaw, he said, which the islanders call the 'eight-day sickness'.

Being a trained doctor myself, I asked if I might assist

at Mary Mckinnon's labour. Mackay told me in no uncertain terms that I was not to interfere. Mrs Mckinnon gave birth to a boy, Lachlan, on the first of the month. The women said the date was a good omen. Then we watched on helpless as he sickened.

There was very little I could do for him. Several times, I fed him a few drops of wine in water on a spoon. He fixed his sea-blue eyes on me and looked at me intently, as though asking a question. On the seventh day, his jaw slackened. On the eighth, with appalling inevitability, he died. I don't know how the parents bear it, to see any increase in their family stymied in this way. Siblings born one after the other go into the same graves. There's a man here told me he's lost nine children. And with every infant death, hope for future generations is diminished.

Forgive me. I have blathered on. I have too much time for rumination and too few to confide in. I hope to post these letters soon, when the first steamer lands, and to have news of you.

***

You are the church font, absorbing dank sorrow into your stone pores. In the front pew, the mother stifles her whimpering sounds, the father twists his cap in his hands. The dour Reverend's voice falters, this time. He is moved. 'Man flourisheth as a flower in the field. For as soon as the wind goeth over it, it is gone, and the place thereof shall know it no more.' Forevermore, you think. The place thereof shall remember it forevermore.

You are the wooden cradle. Stripped of your bedding. Put amongst crates and ropes in a drafty storage cleit. Too short, it was. You were attuned to his every sound and move. The warm weight of him. For a while, you dream phantom cries.

***

I made it out the other side of winter. Just about. The tempests here are a crashing disturbance in the brain, enough to drive a man half mad. I've seen roof tiles blown off in gales and driven into the earth like axe blades. And the endless, malicious rain. It falls in sheets.

Norman Gillies showed me how to ascertain from the flight patterns and calls of birds when a storm is heading our way. He's always right. When it's bad, the children are carried bodily to school by their parents so they aren't blown off the edge. Several sheep meet this fate every year. I learned that the verb 'to die' on Hirta translates as 'to go over it'.

We're past the worst of it now. The oystercatchers arrived this week, and with them the stirrings of spring. We've had four days without rain and even a spell of sunshine! In such sultry weather, when I can roam about the place, I feel the luckiest man on earth. It has done something to me, to see big skies every day. In Edinburgh, you see slivers of the heavens between buildings when you crane your neck to look up. But how often does one look up? We are here so briefly and we see such little of the wondrous world.

***

You are a blade of grass. Bending in the wind on Conachair, a dizzyingly high peak. The land shears away below and the sea stretches in every direction, into eternity, reflecting glittering sunlight like a dimpled pane. Over to the east, a pod of dolphins. The sky has been cloudless all day. Blue, blue, blue. The teacher came to sit here earlier. He laid down his jacket and reclined over you. Thrilling to feel anything other than pummeling rain or the hard pinioning of a sheep's foot. It went dark and you felt the pressure and warmth of his back. You heard his thoughts. He was saying, 'God created every living thing with which the water teems and every winged bird according to its kind.' He was all joy for a moment, thinking of the miracle he looked upon and how it came to be. But he couldn't let his pure thought of God go unstained by that which followed, of the Reverend John Mackay. His whole being became sour. *A single rotten apple infects the whole barrel.* Then his thoughts turned inwards. To his own intrusion into something unspoiled. When he left, it took you hours to stand up. Now the sky is melting into a thousand streaked colours. Lurid pinks you've never seen anywhere else. Down by the houses is a line of people. A long line, processing steadily along the shadow of the setting sun, and at its head a coffin fit for a lamb.

***

You are the lover's stone. A tall pinnacle worn by rain and scrambling feet, infused with the same question repeated over centuries. 'May I have her for marriage?'. You almost always give your blessing.

You are the Great Auk's egg. You have no notion of what an ornithologist is. You merely exist as you are, delicate marbled casing around a ribcage around a beating heart. Impassive. The size of an outstretched palm.

***

May God preserve me. I have exchanged cross words with Mackay. When I told him I planned to leave my books behind for Alex, he spoke rudely to me and told me I would do no such thing. He went further and forbade all teaching materials other than the Bible. No poetry. No history or natural science. I despair. The man is a hindrance to the progress and happiness of the people.

Unfortunately, they are in his thrall. I am just returned from the third interminable sermon of the Sabbath. The third! The islanders were gifted a heater for the church but decided it shouldn't be used- Mackay encourages discomfort. He is a hair-shirt type of man- and it now sits rusting cheerfully on the ground outside. My posterior is positively numbed. He has also deemed it sinful to laugh, smile, play games or do any kind of work on the Sabbath. I am forced to attend his sermons, for if I didn't I would be shunned, and so I curse my gloomy Sundays. The so-called 'day of rest'!

***

You are the discarded church heater. A symbol of mortification, slowly eroding out of usefulness. What's so wrong with comfort, you wonder, as the grass grows tall around you.

You're a shelter made of stacked stones, standing sentinel with the others in Gleann Mor. Ancient. A decade passes in a blink. Warm currents of the past are borne on the breeze and they slip through your gaps, play through the upturned ribs of a nearby sheep's carcass. Only you know how old you are. You're a clue. A trace. But a memory stirs deep within you. A time when fire made your walls glow warm and sinless people slept under your roof.

***

13th June, 1885
My dear friend,

This will be my final missive from St Kilda. I leave in a fortnight.

I have wondered what I have achieved, though the Ladies' Association have written to say they are pleased with me. They asked whether I would consider staying on another year. If it weren't for Mackay, I might have.

Having been cut off from humanity for eight months, since April we have received multiple steamers. They bring supplies, mail and tourists, who really are a menace. One just went by my window, parasol in hand, and peered right at me. The islanders do a roaring trade in tweed and mittens, which they lay out on their doorsteps as soon as they see a mast on the horizon. They have sensed their opportunity and now ask for money for the smallest transaction, capitalism being a relatively new concept to them. The more this place is exposed to mankind's so-called civilising influences, the more it is corrupted. I include myself in this. Tourists have taught them greed and brought over illness. Mackay has taught them shame. I have taught them, of all impractical things, rudimentary English.

I will miss my students and the friends I've made. When they wave me off on the shoreline it may well be my last sight of them on this earth. But I sense I have intruded too long. Now that I have determined to leave, I'm engulfed by a wave of homesickness.

I wish the next schoolmaster luck. He will need it! And if I never see another preserved egg it will be too soon.

***

You are the moth again. Inside a low-ceilinged room at the teacher's farewell gathering, clinging to the fold of a short curtain.

The singing is loud. 'Hymns only. Forget the old songs', Mackay decreed years ago. But he's not here to object. He declined the invitation and sits in the manse, brooding. The dancing thrums through your body. You witness the whisky taken out from the wall and passed round. The honour of mutton, cooked especially. The door is thrown open. It frames the view over Village Bay, casually astonishing.

The teacher entrusts his books to the boy called Alex. 'No need to tell him. Keep them close', he says. Then, 'Keep this. And these. You'll get more use from them than I.' Steadily emptying the packed trunk, handing out pencils and tobacco and his best coat.

Nearly midnight, the gloaming fading fast. You can perceive the spinning of the world here. The full moon is a full-beam spotlight reflecting pearlescent off the sea. A girl sings the final song. The Bird Song. She mimics the wheeling and whistling of seabirds. The verses their chattering, the chorus their calls. *Hin da-la hor-or-hee! Hin da-la-la!* How can anybody make such a sound? It flows from her ancestors out of her mouth. She sings it as a gift.

You take off and lurch towards the open door. In a puff of powder from your wings, you twist and you're a fulmar. Up you go into a vast navy canopy speckled with stars, leaving the row of houses and the people within them far beneath you. Getting smaller. Disappearing. A speck, a pinprick-sized mote. But the girl's song goes on, soaring up with you.

Hoh-ror-ui! Hoh-ror-ui!

You join in. I'm alive! I'm alive!
Snatches of a joyful song, borne away on the breeze.

Historical note: Dr Kenneth Campbell, the first dedicated schoolmaster on St Kilda, was present on the island at a time of great change. 45 years later, the people would vote to be evacuated to the mainland. His obituary states that he was a man of 'grit and perseverance' and 'a delightful raconteur of his reminiscences of […] St Kilda.'

For thousands of years before the islanders were exposed to organised religion, they adhered to animism, a belief system in which all living and non-living things are thought to have a spiritual essence or soul.

It has been posited that the 'eight-day sickness' (tetanus) could have been caused by the fulmar oil used to anoint umbilical cords or by its storage conditions. 61% of all babies born on St Kilda 1856-91 died within the first 27 days of life.

The traditional 'St Kilda Bird Song', after which this story is named, is preserved on the album 'Treasures of Scotland' (1987), sung by Joan Mackenzie. A lively reinterpretation can be heard on Garefowl's 'Cliffs' (2020) https://garefowl.co.uk/music.

HIGHLY COMMENDED
Liz Kershaw

About the Author

Liz Kershaw writes short and long fiction, often with a historical setting. She has won three national short story competitions and has been shortlisted four times for the Historical Writers Association short story award. Her short stories have been selected for various anthologies – including *The Bedford Short Story Competition anthology*, 2014 (with her winning story *Lures*), *The Dorothy Dunnett/Historical Writers Association Short Story Anthologies* (2019 and 2021), *What Haunts the Heart, Songs for the Elephant Man* and *Triptych Tales*.

Most recently, her short story *Intersection* was published in *Night Time Economy* (Floodgate Press, 2024), and *The Drover* was published by Tindal Street Fiction Group in the *Thursday Nights* anthology (2023). Her Gothic novella, *The Music Maker*, was published by Mantle Lane Press in 2018 and in 2019 she was the project writer for the Heritage Lottery-funded community project, *Our Man in the Moone*, reimagining in prose and script the first science fiction novel to be written in English (*The Man in the Moone*, Francis Godwin, 1638).

Her work-in-progress is a volume of linked historical short stories which will be out on submission to agents next year.

Liz is a member of the West Midlands Writing Room 204 scheme for the best emerging regional writers and has performed at the Birmingham Literature Festival. She is also a member of the Tindal Street Fiction Group. Liz lives with her husband in Herefordshire and gains inspiration for her writing from walking in the countryside and visiting sites of historical interest.

www.lizkershaw.co.uk
email: liz@lizkershaw.co.uk

AFTER JUTLAND, 1916
by Liz Kershaw

Portsmouth is bright with the hard, glittering light of sun over sea. The Dockyard throws out sounds of men and machines: chains hauled along the quay, boats' engines roaring into life, cartwheels on cobbles, shouts and laughter, the bellow of a warning horn. Coal smoke frays up from chimneys along red brick terraces, horse dung steams, the door of the Victoria and Albert opens and a bucket of beery water sloshes into the street.

Through it all, Helen Burden clips along, buttoned boots shining, hat, big as a meat plate, lifting in the October breeze. It's almost noon and she's late, has had barely ten minutes to take off her Dockyard overdress and cap, put on her smartest clothes. Appear respectable, the other widows had told her. Watch what you say. None of your attitude. Advice had come at her from all those who'd already faced the War Pensions Committee. Who'd been judged as deserving enough to be given a few Government shillings after the drowning of their men four months before.

A boy runs past her, stripped to his combinations, and jumps into the harbour mud amid whoops from the lads already there. One boy has found a coin, holds it up in triumph. A passer-by shouts, 'scavengers, should be ashamed of yourselves', and the mudlarks jeer back at him. One turns round and sticks out his filthy backside. Another, much smaller, stands, looking lost. Helen spares the little one a glance, feels pity rise and squashes it. Tough. She will have to be tough now to survive and pity is a thing of the past. The church clock strikes, and she quickens her pace. Fred, she thinks, Fred, what did you have to go and die for?

'You should be aware,' the first woman says, 'that the Widow's Pension can be revoked at any time.'

Helen blinks. *Revoked. At any time.* The air has been thick with words in the quarter hour she has spent in this stuffy office, and she has scarcely registered any of them until now. She can't recall the names of her interrogators, two women and two men. She is befuddled by the strings of initials describing this fund or that, everything jumbling up in her mind like the autumn leaves eddying into untidy heaps along the street outside.

'Revoked,' the first woman says again.

The second woman inclines slightly over the table towards Helen. 'Stopped,' she says, in the manner an adult might talk to an uncomprehending child. 'It can be stopped.'

The quartet behind the polished table nod their heads in agreement and regard Helen with impersonal scrutiny. The two men wear black suits that have dampened in the rain and the wet wool is giving off a whiff of lanolin and ingrained cigar smoke. The women are fragrant with cologne and talcum. Expensive smells. Helen's head swims a little. She stares down at her skirt and tries to focus on what they are saying. They have granted her no money yet but are already talking about taking it away.

She'd chosen to wear her decent black taffeta skirt, her fancy blouse with its tiers of creamy lace, her special hat, shiny ebony crepe-de-chine trimmed with white roses, but she realises now as she looks towards the other women that she is completely wrong for this occasion: showy, cheap-looking and old-fashioned. The women opposite wear dainty hats, subdued in size and colour to reflect the national war effort, sober clothing immaculately tailored in the finest fabric.

The first woman stares at Helen, a line pinching between her eyes. Her gaze drifts from the exuberant hat down past lacy frills to the stiff taffeta sheen. Helen's chair has been placed away from the table, marooned; the woman has a clear view of all Helen's excesses.

The woman clears her throat. 'Mrs Burden. You have three boys, we understand. Four, six and eight.'

'Yes Ma'am.'

'Are they fine, vigorous boys, Mrs Burden?'

Helen thinks of Ed and Arthur, her first and last, Ed always climbing trees, winning the races; Arthur, still only four but stronger than most older lads. She thinks of Jess, six, and her answer sticks in her throat. Not that the woman seems to need a response, she is continuing on regardless, like a Dreadnought in full steam.

'Can you assure us that you will bring your boys up as decent and patriotic citizens, proud of their father and of his sacrifice? Boys who will make the Empire proud one day?'

Helen nods.

'Mrs Burden?'

'Yes.' A whisper. She can feel herself being thinned by the slice of their cut-glass consonants, the unsparing regard of their well-bred eyes.

'Nonetheless, you will be monitored to ensure that you are demonstrating responsible mothering of your boys and that you are adhering to all correct standards of personal conduct, morality and sobriety. You will not cohabit or remarry and if you do, your pension will be revoked. And finally, we will expect you to find employment and not rely solely upon the beneficence of the state and charitable organisations. Your pension is a gratuity linked to

Able Seaman Burden's patriotic service. It is not an automatic right regardless of behaviour. Do you understand?'

'Yes,' Helen says. 'Yes.' And all the things she would like to say race up through her like the explosion that killed her Fred on HMS Black Prince, and she swallows, hard, because for a woman like her speaking her mind is not a choice she will ever be allowed to make.

'Thank you,' she says, 'I am very,' the word snags, she tries again, 'I am most grateful.' She can see the expression on the beefier man's face soften, but then his gaze lingers on the swell of her bust just a little too long. She dips her head, her expression shrouded in the shadow of her hat.

At home, later, her sister Lizzie calls in with a fresh-baked loaf and a packet of chitterlings from the butcher, and homes in on the white space on the wall.

'Where's that photograph gone? The studio one of you and Fred?'

'I've put it away,' Helen says. 'In the chest in the bedroom.'

'Why?'

'Fred's gone. I can't be doing with remembering all the time, it'll weaken me.'

'What on earth would Fred think of that, being stuffed there in the dark and forgotten?'

'Fred can't think anything, he's at the bottom of the North Sea.' Helen picks up the chitterlings and slams them, packet and all, into the meat safe. All her life, she's been on a see-saw with Lizzie, one always slightly higher than the other, and now Lizzie is married and up, and Helen is widowed and down. And that's how it will be for the rest of their days. She's grateful for the loaf and the meat, just as she was grateful for the tea and sugar the week before. Just as she will be grateful for the Pension and any scraps of charity that come her way. She sees a lifetime of gratitude stretching ahead of her and says with a flash of her old spirit, 'And anyway, I reckon Fred wouldn't have minded the thought of spending eternity wrapped up inside my drawers.'

Once upon a time Lizzie would have laughed at that. Now, she has an older sister face on even though she's the younger by a year. 'You be careful, Helen Burden, do you hear? You're too outspoken. That could be taken as unsuitable talk, and you don't want any consequences.'

'What I don't want is you telling me what to do.'

Lizzie huffs. 'Only trying to help.'

'And I'm very grateful, I'm sure.'

Lizzie tuts and tells her she is too outspoken for her own good, and Helen thanks her for the food and opens the door. She hasn't offered Lizzie a cup of tea, and Lizzie doesn't ask. Helen watches her sister pick her way over the cobbles of the back yard, duck under the washing line, stalk past the privy and out of the gate. The gate swings shut, bangs against the post. It's as if Lizzie's leaving has sucked the noise and life away and all that is left is the absence of Fred. Outspoken, Lizzie had said, but Helen's voice has withered since the afternoon in the Town Hall. She has been made slighter; there is less to her now that her husband is no more.

She imagines Lizzie's boots stomping down the road and carrying on further into Portsea Island where their mother runs a boarding house. Lizzie will tell their mother that Helen is her own worst enemy, and their mother will agree and say that Helen was always difficult, and they'll make a cup of tea and wonder what to do with her.

Helen goes to the biscuit tin where she keeps her money and tots up what will be left after the rent man comes, and she's paid her tally at the grocer. Lizzie's bread sits fatly on the bread board succulent and fragrant. Helen picks it up, inhales deep as her lungs will allow, puts it down and goes out to call the boys for their tea.

Helen had found no chance to tell the women and the men who had sat in judgement on her that she has already gained employment, is not relying solely on the charity of anyone. After Fred died, Lizzie had told her that there was work for women down at the Dockyard. Now that there is conscription, men are thin on the ground. There had always been a few women employed in the colour loft, making flags, or in the office, typing or copying. Now, they are wanted in the areas where men had reigned unchallenged: welding, buffing, drilling, engraving, woodturning – dirty tasks, heavy tasks, tasks that fill a gap and earn the women money. Jutland widows were being favoured, Lizzie said, and so Helen had applied and has been a Triangle Girl for three months with a cap and an overdress and a Triangle badge saying, 'On War Service'. 'It's not right,' her mother had said, 'working at those dirty jobs close up with men,' but she'd agreed anyway to help with Helen's boys, giving them their tea, minding Arthur who was too young for school.

The day after her interview with the panel, Helen returns home with oil smudges on her face and fingers ingrained with the muck of shipbuilding. Her shoulders ache with the lifting she has done all day, her hair itches with sweat. Her mother is at the sink, rinsing dishes. Lizzie is there too, drying. Helen comes in the back door, and they stare at her askance.

'You look like a hoyden dragged through a hedge,' her mother says.

'So would you if you'd been drilling holes in steel all day,' Helen says, and sits heavily on a kitchen chair. 'It's needs must, you know that.'

Lizzie, apparently keen on détente with Helen, nods.

Her mother fills a kettle, thumps it on the range, turns to face her. It's a funny kind of love, this anger in her mother, this lack of tenderness, but Helen knows it is love. The sort of love that tries to forge resilience in a child, strength that will be needed day in, day out for the rest of its life. Tough. Being soft, her mother would say, had never got anyone anywhere.

'Your Jess,' her mother begins.

'What about him?'

'Do you - ' even her mother stumbles at the question.

'Do I think he's all there?' The words hang, stark and ugly, across the scrubbed table.

The other two women say nothing. Lizzie has three children like Helen, all of them big and strong, winners like Ed and Arthur. This is the pattern they all know. The oddity of Jess foxes them.

'I don't know,' Helen says, and lays her grimy head on her arms. 'I just don't know. He's as big as the others but he can't climb like they do – he falls off, bumps into things. And he can't read. Ed says the teacher is always pulling him out and sticking him in the corner. Asks him what's on the board and he hasn't a clue. And yet he's sharp enough with his questions and learns things if you tell him.' Her eyes prick, and she bites, hard, into her lip.

Her mother makes tea, and they drink it, keep off the subject of Jess, talk about how the other women who had lost their husbands at Jutland are managing. In the next street along, seventeen women had been widowed overnight on that last fatal day in May. Portsmouth had taken the brunt of the Battle of Jutland losses. Fourteen ships had been sunk at Jutland. Over six thousand men had died and their women and children left behind to grieve. Some of the widows are working with Helen at the Dockyard, some are getting by with piecework here and there. A few have given up, sent their children to orphanages or family members, or fallen to drink to escape. One was found hanging in the woods.

When her mother and sister have gone, Helen takes off the overdress and shakes off the metal filings, brushes out her sweaty, oily hair. Lizzie has brought another loaf, but there is only a heel of cheese and a jar of jam in the cupboard to go with it. Helen cuts the bread, three slices spread with jam. The biggest for Ed, the next for Arthur, the smallest one for Jess. This is how the animals do it, she thinks, and pushes the tears away.

A month on, November, and Jess has started refusing to go to school. 'I get hit,' he says, 'I don't want to go. I shan't.'

Helen tries everything: she smacks, cajoles, threatens, bribes, but still Jess sits at the kitchen table, mulish, his hair with its wayward widow's peak echoing his stiff unhappy little face.

'Shan't,' he says, and in the end, she leaves him there and goes off to her work, racing along the dusty streets, past the Devil's Acre packed with public houses, in through the great Dockyard gate. Her life is beginning to unravel, she thinks, into threads of hunger, not making ends meet, trying to manage the boys and work – and now Jess, odd and difficult, soaring out of control. He's no good, she thinks. He won't amount to anything, and I need to be tough. Look to the strong ones. And each week, she feeds Ed and Arthur a little more, and Jess's portion grows a little smaller.

It takes a week for the school attendance officer to arrive. His circuit of visits has taken him to the red brick infants with its brass bell and paved playground two streets away from Helen's house. It's the school Helen had gone to, where she had met Fred, the school to where Ed goes off happily in his grey shorts and battered black boots, ready to do battle with anyone. And to where Jess is refusing to go at all. She has been notified of the appointment, has to beg leave from the Dockyard and is home in plenty of time to put a cloth on the gateleg table in the parlour, and prepare her best china to win the man over with a cup of tea.

He is a young man, slight, with a wispy moustache and a pigeon chest that rattles when he breathes. She suspects he has been turned down for active service and this is the best work of patriotism he has been able to find: rounding up lost boys and chastising their parents. He is unmoved by the cup and saucer laid on a tray, the sugar in its bowl, sponge fingers lined on a plate. He declines the offer of tea, stands apart and aloof, refusing, even, the invitation to enter Helen's neat little parlour. They remain in the kitchen, Helen by the sink and the attendance officer so close to the range that she thinks he might singe his trousers.

'Your son Jess has not been attending school, Mrs Burden.'

'I know,' Helen says. 'He's unhappy. He's behind, and he's always in trouble, so he runs away.'

'The point is not why he runs away, but how will you ensure that he does not run away?'

Helen comes out with the answer she has rehearsed: potential punishments, help from her mother but her words are like water on oilcloth and the man's face shows no change.

'Do you know where he goes when he is not at school?'

She hesitates. When she presses Jess, he clams up, and really, she has no idea. 'He,' she starts, but gets no further. There is a clatter of boots hitting the cobbles in the yard, the door swings open and bashes against the wall, and Jess runs in, pulling up short at the sight of his mother and the man. At least, she assumes it is Jess. It is a boy of Jess's size and shape, but it is caked in mud from top to toe, the brown oily sludge of Portsmouth Harbour left behind when the tide goes out.

Helen gasps and holds onto the sink for support. The school attendance officer remains impassive.

'I think that question has just been answered,' he says. 'Mudlarking. Tell me,' he turns to Helen, 'are you sending your son out to scavenge for you?'

'How could you?' she screams at Jess when the man has gone. 'That man will tell the Pensions Committee, I know he will, and then that'll be it, no money, no food for any of us. They'll say I'm a bad mother.'

Jess says nothing. Just that look on his face. Stubborn.

She tries again. 'Why, Jess? I know you're not happy at school but surely it's better than spending all day in stinking harbour mud?' He shrugs. She looks at his clothes in confusion. Under the mud is an outfit of shirt and short trousers that she has never seen before. 'Where did you get those?'

'I took them off a washing line. I keep them in the coal shed.'

'So you've stolen clothes to go mudlarking – you've been mudlarking every day? And what, sluicing yourself down in the yard when you get back?'

He nods.

'It's no good,' she says, and her voice is flat with despair. 'I can't let you wreck your brothers' lives. We need that pension money. I'm going to have to send you to live somewhere else and then maybe I can persuade the committee to give me another chance.'

She waits for him to argue but he is silent. 'Go on,' she says, 'and get yourself cleaned up. I've got some thinking to do.' When she turns back, he is still standing by the wall, his small figure cased in stiffening mud, runnels of tears starting to track down his face. *I must be tough*, she thinks, as she sends a telegram to her aunt in Deptford asking if she'll take Jess to help her out. *I must be tough*, as she packs Jess's few things up in her old carpet bag. *I must be tough* as she lays out tea for the boys that night and gives them equal portions. *I must be tough* as she puts Jess on the train to London with a label round his neck and the heavy bag dragging on the ground. *I must be tough* as she goes home and sets the table for two boys, and not three.

'Where's Jess?' Ed asks that night, and she tells him Jess has gone to London for a holiday. Ed purses his lips. She sees that he is pondering the justice of a holiday for Jess whereas he has to go to school.

'Has he gone to London to get some spectacles?' Ed asks.

'Spectacles? No, why?' It is such an unexpected

question she stares at him.

'Because they tested our eyes at school last month and he was meant to tell you he needed spectacles. It's why he can't read. He can't see the blackboard.'

'No', she says, 'he didn't say a thing.'

Helen imagines Jess trying to think of the words to tell her he needed spectacles – the cost of them, how she might have reacted. In reflex, she goes to her money tin and opens it, expecting to find it empty, but to her surprise, there are coins in it, enough to buy a bit of cheese and bacon. She frowns, perplexed. Then, puts her hand in, pulls out a few coins, lays them on the tablecloth. They are dulled by use but there is something else. Something unusual. She peers closer, scratches at the surface of one, and looks at her fingernail, at its tiny scraping of Portsmouth harbour mud.

HIGHLY COMMENDED
Elaine O'Connor

About the Author

Inspiration is eclectic. The dip-pen thrust into my hand by a teacher telling me to write a composition. Surely, *What I did in the Holidays?* The note-book gifted by my daughter, aged 12: *To Mum, lots of love, Rachel, for your poetry etc.* A photograph of my Mum, 17, a newly-qualified nurse in the 1930s. My son, Alex, persistently encouraging me to enter writing competitions - *If you don't shoot, Mum, you never score.* James Baldwin's advice - Write a sentence as clean as a bone - despatched the florid from my work.

If *What I did in the Holidays* started me, it was a lonely affair for many years. Creative writing courses in the 1970s were known and accessible to vanishingly few.

Access to the internet, and owning my own laptop were transformational. Writing associations, courses, magazines and competitions poured through the ether, crashing through the door of my imaginary garret under the eaves. In marched myth-makers, world-creators and shape-shifters, inspiring stories, poetry, flash-fiction, novels. That dip-pen has never been repudiated in favour of the keyboard. I feel it still, between my finger and thumb, as my hands hover over the keyboard.

My first long work, an unpublished novel, *The Long Road Home*, relates women's arduous experiences of the 1930's Irish diaspora, through my protagonist, Bridie Nolan.

My work sometimes flows effortlessly, sometimes

churns. My creativity is sustained by Chiltern Writers Group, and its off-shoot Manuscript Review Group, the Nitpickers, who allow no infelicities to pass unchallenged.

elaineoconnor089@gmail.com

NO COMPETITION
by Elaine O'Connor

A hard little nut of a thing was Nora Noakes, a conker of a girl, round-faced, stout-calved and stocky. Boys dribbling footballs in the playground, reliving the heroics of Reg Lewis in the FA Cup Final, swerved respectfully around her. Knots of girls skipped or played hopscotch, and if they did not beckon her to join in, nor did they tease her.

The overcrowded Junior School in which I taught had been knocked about by generations of children, like an old friend who no longer notices the daily thumps of greeting long ago grow too rough. Victorian entrances for Girls and Boys remained at either end of the building, looking over the grey asphalt playground.

And Nora Noakes read.

Sitting on an upturned milk-crate in the summer or squashed under the lintel of a classroom door in winter, Nora Noakes read. Her lips moved, her hands gestured, her body swayed as she whispered life into the words. If she wanted for the company of other children, she never showed it. She did not eye their activities enviously, nor hover at the edges of games, waiting to be noticed. A mutual understanding prevailed. Nora was accepted, even admired for the loner she was, and none of her classmates interfered with that.

She was my favourite, a relationship that neither then, nor now, would be countenanced. When I asked her to read aloud, an effortlessly expressive voice rose from her rotund, immature chest. Her classmates were grateful for the break from multiplication tables, learning dates by heart or copying joined-up writing scripts with ill-designed dip-pens whose nibs always worked loose, splattering Quink over their efforts. Yet even their usual eagerness for a lull in boring schoolwork could not completely account for the rapt attention Nora commanded. In the dingy cream and green classroom, they listened as if she had stepped out of a fairy-ring to speak to them.

Junior 4th's poetry curriculum followed dull, irrelevant texts set by middle-class men with no idea of the reality of urban life in a pit-town. Raggle taggle gypsies, The Ducks' Ditty, I remember, I remember. Doggerel, these poems that now fill popular anthologies and are constantly requested on radio shows. The nation's favourites...

'What's a roach, miss?' Stacy asked.

'What's a ditty, for that matter?' Billy chimed in.

The children used laughter to cover their confusion at these unfamiliar rural, middle-class worlds, seen only in idealised textbook illustrations. 'I remember, I remember,' had little resonance for impoverished young townies with neither experience nor understanding of its imagery. Sandra, whose garden consisted of a grubby yard, home to her dad's and brothers' motorbikes, asked if people really had gardens with flowers made of light; and if they did, well how could they pick them then? I told her we'd look in the park next time we had a nature ramble to find things for the table that stood at the side of the class, usually home to stones, twigs, pine cones and conkers. She looked rightly sceptical, so I brought in some honesty instead, and held it up to the window to show how the seed-pods glowed with sunlight shining through.

Why do people have fond memories of this poetry? Is it all that is left of the mythic childhood that preceded the pit-cage, the drunken one-night stand that precipitated a hopeless marriage, the ankle-swelling hours serving behind the high wooden counters at Woolworths? Memories of children like Nora rapping out, 'Guns to the left of them! Guns to the right of them!' exist in an innocence relinquished to the swallowing darkness of the mine, sodden nappies and screaming babies, the endlessly hopeless task of making ends meet.

It transformed Nora, reciting in her too-small, darned frock and plastic shoes, hair greasy in the sunlight through which chalk dust danced. She hardly glanced at the poetry book, instead tipping her head back like a dancer checking her eye-line and reciting without hesitation or self-consciousness. As natural as a leaf unfurling, she captured her vast, imagined audience that stretched through the classroom wall, across the playground, past the mine-shaft and down the hill to town, thousands whose eyes were fixed on her for just those few moments.

Finished, she would stomp back to her desk clutching the unnecessary book, while every eye followed her. I think then, when she had just finished, laying out her simple soul for all to see, many of the children would have spoken, made a friend of her. When the bell clanged for playtime, she was alone again, curled into her book-lined shell.

Lily Sparkes, whose dad was the accountant at the British Coal Board offices and could afford the weekly children's drama club run by the local theatre, was Nora's only rival, yet not really a rival at all. Lily was a sweet, vacant, beautifully spoken child destined to be a secretary or hotel receptionist, or – her great dream – an air hostess, until she married a nice boy and produced sweet, vacant children of her own, on whom she would undoubtedly dote. With none of Nora's rhythm or passion, Lily pronounced and articulated with precision, face alight with a charming smile and no feeling whatever.

'Lips and teeth dear, lips and teeth!' I could hear her drama teacher exhorting. And Lily loved Nora nearly as much as I, though Nora did not know it.

***

The staff meeting lapsed into startled silence when I suggested that Nora recite the finale on the end of year Open Day.

Miss Fairclough, the Reception Teacher, stared at me as if I had suggested that the Nativity be performed in the round in black costumes and skull-masks. Experienced, amused eyes gleamed knowingly at me, the new girl wanting to impress with her sense of social justice. Through the dusty windows behind their phalanx of permed heads, I watched the late mothers gripping tearful stragglers' hands, rebuking them for being so silly. The faces in the Staff Room reflected the same admonishment. I knew exactly how those children felt.

'Nora is a natural,' I stated. 'I don't suggest her because I feel sorry for her or any such nonsense. She's a bright, ardent child with an excellent memory, and totally unselfconscious. She has no nerves once she starts speaking and never forgets a word. She'd recite really well.'

Mrs Hunt, the Deputy Head, flicked her Players cigarette distractedly towards the glass, shell-shaped ash tray, depositing most of the grey dust on the table around it.

'I don't think anyone disagrees with you, dear'.

She glanced round, and the others nodded, murmured, assented: they had all taught Nora in their time, of course.

'But sadly' she continued, exhaling a trail of smoke through her bright pink 'Summer Rose' coated lips, 'she's scruffy. Can't help it, I know. But even a school like this must wear its best bib and tucker for Open Day, especially with Governors in attendance.'

The Headmistress, Mrs Ramsbotham, agreed politely and regretfully with her Deputy. She had heard Nora recite when inspecting one of my early, nervous classes. She did not doubt the girl's ability, of course, she made it clear. But her appearance, while it could not be helped, was a drawback. The parents were decent, hard-working folk of their kind. She hated to think what on earth they were going to do when Nora passed the 11-plus exam, as she undoubtedly would, and found they could not afford the uniform or the bus fare to the Girls Grammar in the next town. But all that aside, Nora would not reflect well, not well at all. Perhaps she might be encouraged in other ways, do something else on Open Day?

'But little Lily Sparkes, now...' Mrs Hunt declared and that was the end of the matter. Bright, clean, well-spoken Lily would recite Edgar Guest's Don't Quit, the school's traditional final piece, in which the parental audience loved to join.

I managed to plaster a bright smile on my face and say nothing.

***

Nora was late leaving that day. She usually rushed off to help at home, but she was scrabbling in her draw-string bag, frowning, when I returned defeated from the staff room.

'What is it, Nora?' I asked. 'Have you lost something?'

'Yes Miss. My book Miss. It's gone Miss.'

She was frantic.

'I see. Well, let's look together, shall we? What book is it? When did you last have it?'

'Palgrave. Golden Tre'sry. Lunch-time.'

If my mouth rounded in astonishment, I could only hope she was too distracted to notice. We had no such book in the school. Her parents could not afford it and she had no older siblings who might have brought it home from secondary school.

It had slipped behind the bookcase that stood at the back of the class. As I helped her repack her bag to fit it in, I asked her where it came from.

'Lib'ry Miss.'

'You go to the one in town?'

I was touched that her parents would scrimp enough for the bus fare.

'No Miss. Trav'lin. Comes up our street once a fortnight. I've had a ticket for ages and never, ever had a fine.'

She paused, then confided,

'The lady, the librarian, she gets me books special sometimes. Things she thinks I'd like. Long stories. 'Children of the New Forest.' 'What Katy Did,' things like that. Poetry. Hard books', the last said with great pride.

'That's kind of her Nora' I smiled. 'I'm glad. No wonder you were worried though, dear.'

Without thinking, I placed my hand on her grubby little arm. She looked at me, astonished, then smiled.

'I was, Miss, but I got it now.'

'So, you have.'

I hesitated.

'What's your favourite poem then, Nora?'
She took a deep breath, sniffed and looked hesitant.
'No tellin'?'

'Cross my heart and hope to die.'

She laughed with as much with delight at my use of the childish promise, as if I had transformed into a parrot before her eyes.

'"Goblin Market". I like the story and Lizzie being so brave as to save her sister. But I like "Overheard on a salt marsh" as well, because that goblin is wicked, wicked. Mean and grasping. And the nymph tells him, 'No!'. Just like that.'

Her voice rose with the drama of the poetry, and she curled her lips and fists to demonstrate the goblin's envy, howling to demonstrate how he lay in the mud, coveting the moon beads. Then she thanked me, said she was ever so glad to have her book back, and hurried away.

'Mum will be wondering where I am.'

I stared after her.

***

Through the hot summer of Junior 4th's last term, we practised country dancing, gym displays and folk songs. Mothers sewed costumes; fathers stacked staging and seating, set out chairs, checked and oiled the creaking workings of the stage curtains not used since Christmas.

Lily had extra coaching from her drama teacher and practised 'When things go wrong, as they sometimes will,' with sweet expressionlessness in front of her classmates. While she did so, Nora sat reading 'The Chronicles of Robin Hood'. I did not rebuke her because sometimes I saw her look up, her lips moving with words that Lily stumbled over. Sometimes, when Lily floundered to a halt, the children would look at me through the dust motes sliding in the light, then turn to look at Nora and back to me.

Billy Fairclough, captain of the school football team, which was to prove his proudest achievement in life, stopped beside me one stifling afternoon as I supervised the children's routine on the vaulting horses.

His panted message was short, sharp, clear.

'Nora. It should be Nora, Miss. Or at least Nora as well as Lily,' then he ran off to join the back of the line about to start on their cartwheels.

After all the children had finished their compositions that day, I clapped my hands for silence.

'Nora,' I instructed, 'you will please read or recite for us, 'Overheard on a Salt Marsh'. Let us give Lily a well-deserved break.'

I fixed Billy with a gimlet stare, and he gazed back, all wide-eyed innocence, while the boys around him grinned.

Lily could not have looked more relieved nor Nora more irritated, despite the huge smile that Lily bestowed on her. Nora knew a booby prize when she was handed one.

Nonetheless, she took up her stance in front of my desk and declaimed to a photograph of Princess Elizabeth on the far classroom wall.

Puffed clouds floated across the summer sky. The sun soured the left-over milk in its glass bottles in the crate. The breeze sighed through the half open sash windows. Children cupped their chins in their hands or folded their arms on their desks to rest their heads. Billy tipped his chair back to lean on the desk behind him and grinned. I did not, as usual, tell him sharply to sit on his chair properly, this instant.

Nora's voice floated out into the silence of the long, childhood, summer's afternoon, conjuring the reedy marshes and mocking nymph, in calm control as the goblin danced and spat his avariciousness at her. She howled his fury and distress, and the nymph's clipped, triumphant refusal.

***

Parents always looked different on Open Days, their usual tiredness and fluster rubbed away by cold flannels and replaced by Sunday best. Mothers wore floral, cotton frocks in place of nylon overalls. The very few dads, in open-necked shirts, hoped for an early departure to the pub.

The children danced, sang, jumped and performed with giggling enthusiasm, aware of proud eyes on them. Prizes were given, cups presented, captains commended and thanks liberally dispensed. With outdoor activities done, the Headmistress and Governors rose augustly to lead everyone inside for the last recitations and music concert.

I had not seen Mrs. Noakes, always so faithful to her tubby little girl, all the afternoon. I'd presumed that she would come to see Nora presented with her 'Commendation for Composition' certificate, but it was too late for that now.

In the stuffy hall, walls were festooned with examples of the children's best work, pinned to cork boards. The children were becoming restless in the heat. They had led their parents through decorated classrooms, pointing at all they had crafted: pictures trimmed with red card, potato prints on scarves and handkerchiefs, cross-stitched table mats, woven cane potholders: simple wooden dish racks and trinket boxes. They had exhibited all they possibly could and wanted to go home now to spam sandwiches and lemonade, the real start of the holidays. But they met the final demands of the day and settled to let their companions have their moments of glory too. Recorders tweeted, violins squeaked, and pianos rang out. The choir piped out a final, disharmonious rendition of 'D'ye Ken John Peel?' and little Charlie Matthews sang his last solo before secondary modern thumped his love of music and other such nonsense out of him.

Lily was the last to step onto the stage, uniform starched and pressed, hair beribboned and white sandals pristine. She was such a sweet, happy, guileless child and thrummed out her poem to her parents' glowing pride.

As she slid with faultless articulation and expressionless charm toward the last verse, as the audience enthusiastically joined in, a hand tapped my arm, Billy, still red-faced from the gym display. He jerked a thumb over his shoulder. Mrs Noakes stood panting against the rear wall of the hall, a tiny baby dozing on her shoulder. Mr Noakes, in oil-stained overalls stood beside her, a twin toddler on each arm. They looked fondly at Nora as she waved and held up her certificate for them to see.

'Sorry, love,' her Mum mouthed at her.
Billy shook my arm.
'Nora, Miss. Please Miss – Nora.'
Junior 4 had all turned to look at me.

I stood, flew to where Nora sat and gently took the certificate from her hand.

'Nora,' I whispered. 'I need you to recite 'Overheard on a Saltmarsh'. Can you do that for me?'

She regarded me suspiciously as I listened frantically to Lily and the audience reaching the end.

'Yes Miss. But why Miss?'

'Oh - because there's a gap at the end of the programme. You must fill it for me please, or I'll be in trouble.'

'Righto then Miss.'

I grasped her hand and stood, just as Lily walked beaming from the stage as the applause died away, and before the headmistress could move. I walked Nora up the steps to the stage, Lily beaming at us as she walked past.

'Good luck Nora,' she whispered. 'You'll be great.'

***

The Governors stared and began to inspect their purple, roneoed programmes again, muttering under their breath, searching for what they had missed.

'Children, parents, Chairman and Governors,' I said, in a voice dry with nerves. 'I present Nora Noakes who will perform our final piece.'

Junior 4 held their collective breath as the headmistress stood stock-still at the bottom of the steps. I watched my career slide like rain down a storm-drain but held Nora's shoulders gently and pushed her to the front of the stage.

Nora held up her little, round face, locked her eyes on her Mum and Dad, and began. She reached out into the heat of that final afternoon and conjured her magic over the heads of astounded parents and gaping Governors. As her voice faded, and the poem finished – 'No!' - the hall lapsed into silence and I saw, from a great distance, her mother and father smile and lock the picture of their little girl's recital into their memories. I had never seen Mr Noakes smile before.

Nora turned to look at me in the long silence that followed, apprehensive, nervous for the first time I could remember. Nothing happened. No-one moved. It was Mr Sparkes and Lily, looking in astonished delight at each other, who brought down the flood of applause, standing, clapping, shouting.

'Bravo, our Nora. Bravo that girl!'

Junior 4 leapt up behind him, echoing words they had never heard before and were never likely to repeat.

'Bravo our Nora. Bravo that girl!'

I did not lose my job but neither did I ever teach another Nora. Such children are rare, hidden, shining in the grass, and you must move quickly to pick them up and protect them before winter descends. I taught on contentedly, promoted to replace Mrs Hunt, and eventually, I married. I came back to the little school to watch my own girls dance and sing, walk through dusty classrooms to admire their paintings and wonky pottery: then returned to teach again when they moved on to the local Grammar, and eventually to university.

***

One bright, autumn day, as another half-term approached, there was a soft knock at my classroom door.

'Come in – quickly now,' I called in my professional teacher's voice. 'We need to be on our way home really, don't we?'

I didn't look up until a resonant voice said, 'Hello Miss.'

A statuesque young woman, brown hair shining where it curled on her shoulders, dressed in a neat, navy suit, stood in the doorway.

Nora had not languished at secondary modern or become thick-ankled in Woolworth's. No, she told me, sitting on a chair far too small for her, beside my desk. Mr Sparkes had paid for her uniform and equipment for grammar school, on the understanding she would pay it back when she got her first teaching job. He had negotiated a free place for her at the Drama Club, and her friendship with Lily blossomed. Nora baby-sat Lily's children sometimes now, reading them bed-time stories while their fond Mum and Dad went to the pictures or the Berni Inn.

'I came back, Miss, because I wanted to teach here. I knew I wanted it from the day you took me up on that stage, and Mam and Dad saw I could do it. I didn't know it exactly then, but I had a sort of sense of what you risked for me. I did come back to tell you, when I got my place at teacher training college, but you'd left to get married, so I was so pleased to hear you were back now. I start teaching here next term.'

She let out a rich laugh.

'Junior 4,' she smiled. 'I'm teaching Junior 4, Miss. I think I'm obliged to start with "'Is there anyone there?' said the traveller", but I'll sneak in Geoffrey Hill and Dylan Thomas before we're done!'

She wrapped her young, lithe arms around me in an embrace I could not refuse. A hard little nut of a thing, Nora Noakes, grown tall and graceful as a maple in autumn.

SHORTLISTED
Laura Karim

About the Author

Laura is passionate about using fiction to restore the voices of women who have been obscured by the traditional male narratives. She is writing a new series about forgotten medieval women for Sapere Books, with the first novel exploring the life and legacy of Mary de Bohun, and her enduring influence over her husband Henry Bolingbroke (later Henry IV.)

She studied late Medieval England and France at Oxford University, with a particular focus on the Wars of the Roses. She is an alumnus of Curtis Brown Creative's Writing Your Novel Course and was mentored by the historical novelist Suzannah Dunn, and was longlisted in the DDS/HWA short story competition in 2023.

She lives in North London with her husband, son and two cats. Writing is her happy place, which has helped her cope with thyroid cancer.

Follow Laura on X at @LauraAKarim. She can also be contacted through her agent Nicky Lovick at WGM Atlantic.

MOTHER'S FURY
by Laura Karim

June 1381 – London

Some people would have thought it impossible. But I don't. I believe. I know what we can achieve if we stand together and refuse to submit. That's why men follow me.

The gates to the most secure fortress in England swing open and we pour in. I go first, a blade in my hand, my skirts hitched up and torn from days of marching. John follows one step behind, with his blacksmith tools and a huge grin on his face. The men of our company charge after us in their hundreds, bows on their backs and brandishing pitchforks and axes.

We surge down Water Lane towards the White Tower. Its grim bulk has dominated the capital since the Conquest. Kings of France have tried and failed to capture it. Now its guards stand aside for a seamstress from Rochester. They drop their weapons and greet us with cheers and handshakes.
'God's blood, Joanna. You're a marvel.' John laughs. 'How did you persuade them to let us in?'
I shrug. 'Call it feminine guile, if you will, husband.'
Of course, it wasn't. Guards have families too.

They are no different to us, for all they take the King's coin. I have no quarrel with them. They have wives, mothers and children waiting at home, and wondering where their next meal will be coming from after the tax is paid.

The King's laws are not our laws. His taxes are legalised theft, snatching the last loaf from the hands of the sick and dying. His swords are nothing to fear. I will fight them with my own, and win.

Let Wat go to Smithfield and attempt to negotiate if he wants. I won't. He is a fool if he believes their lies.

Pledges extracted under duress mean nothing. I don't want empty promises of pardons and change.

I want justice. Justice for my son. Justice for every mother who has lost a child from hunger.

Yesterday I burnt the Savoy. Lancaster's great palace reduced to ashes. His wine poured into the Thames. His ill-gotten gold confiscated and returned to the common people. Today I've come for the heads of Hales and Sudbury. Nothing else will do.

*

'The King is only fourteen years old,' Wat says. 'He is young, Joanna, we can mould him. Make him into our man. A champion of the Commons.'

'With whom do you hold?' Wat shouts.

'With King Richard and the True Commons,' the men chant in unison.

I disagree.

King Richard is no puppet. He bowed and smiled when he spoke to us at Mile End. Of course, he did. Who wouldn't when confronted with thousands of men wielding bows and billhooks?

I looked into his grey eyes, and I saw an adversary; cold, and calculating. A snake who will say anything to get us to return home.

Clerics tell us the hapless Eve was deceived by

such a creature in God's garden. I have my doubts. I'll wager it was Adam who was duped. As for Wat he is only our leader because he rescued my friends Agnes and Joan, when they were captured and held in chains. He may even have paid the tax if we, mere women, hadn't first refused.

No one granted me my freedom, I tell the bonded men who join our revolt in their thousands. I saw an opportunity and I took it. You must do the same. You don't need grants and charters. What use are they when you can't read what they say? All you need is your own wits and determination. Only a simpleton would trust a man dressed in furs and ermine to understand and sympathise with our poverty. Only a fool is taken in by youth.

At fourteen I escaped from the convent.

A farrier came calling to see to the Abbess's horses. He wore a coat that had seen better days. The sisters thought him unremarkable. Little did they know he would leave with the prime mare and a young novice on the back.

They would have hung him for theft if we had been caught. None would have believed it was all my idea, sweet looking girl that I am, but it was.

We were married the next day and on our way to the battlefields of France the day after. So began my life of freedom.

Our lives were awash with coin and wine as the English chevauchees smashed through fertile countryside, pillaging and raiding. There were elements I didn't care for. Wailing women pursued by drunken men in our regiment. Young children shrieking with hunger. But I learnt to live with it as every soldier's wife must. We had to eat and make a living. In the regiment that wasn't a problem. There were always horses to be reshod, and John's share of the loot. The French became wise to our tactics and our forward charges became sideways crawls with slimmer and slimmer pickings. The war was drawing to a close and we seemed certain to lose. That's when we made the mistake of returning to England.

I was pregnant, and John had romantic notions about our baby being born among the apple orchards of Kent. Didn't I tell you men can be foolish?

Our almond-eyed boy entered the world on the earth floor of the smallholding we leased with our remaining coins. We couldn't afford furniture. The brace of poached pheasants hanging from the ceiling were our most valuable possessions.

The pain of labour was like nothing I had experienced before. Like my body being ripped apart by a pack of wolves. Should they decide I merit a traitor's death for my crimes and draw me forward on a hurdle to Tyburn I can't believe the process will be as long or insidious.

Only loss and grief hurt more. As their loved ones will soon discover.

*

'Go find our enemies.' I raise my fist and address our men. 'You know who we seek.' Hales. Sudbury. Lancaster. 'Bring them to me.'

The men charge up the steep spiral staircase inside the White Tower, where the guards told me our quarry cower. Hales and Sudbury are praying in the chapel, they said. Much good may it do them.

We all know Lancaster is away fighting the Scots, but I like to remind the men of him, and keep their hatred burning as brightly as the smouldering ashes of his palace.

Hales and Sudbury proposed the poll taxes. But it was Lancaster who authorised them in the King's name. Lancaster who wanted to fund wars in France and Scotland, and his own extravagant lifestyle. Lancaster who loses every military expedition he leads. Lancaster whose bailiffs evicted us from our smallholding and killed my boy.

The great oak doors on the first floor of the White

Tower are wide open. Our men pour across the threshold three at a time. I smile and step forward to follow them. The long wait is over. Justice will soon be mine. John grabs my right shoulder. 'Let's wait here,' he hisses, his breath hot against my ear. 'This is the most dangerous moment. The enemy could easily sally out and cut us down while we are hemmed in by the stairs and each other. I've seen it done many times.'

I nod and bite my tongue.

No-one resists, and I know they won't.

The nobles have no stomach for the fight. They only have to look out a casement to know they have lost. Clouds of smoke linger across London blocking out the sun. From the fires we set at the Savoy and the bonfires of legal documents Wat ordered at Temple. Any gentleman with sense has fled.

I don't point this out. John means well. He is thinking of my safety. Better to say nothing and let him play the part of the chivalrous husband.

The last of the men have ascended the staircase. John smiles and squeezes my hand. His blond hair is black with soot, and his clothes reek of smoke. Mine do too. I inhale the scent of retribution and it steadies me. We walk up the steps together. Now is the time.

*

December 1380 – Kent

Lancaster's men came to collect the rent on St Stephen's Day. Ten retainers in chain mail, armed with swords and mounted on fine horses. John and I knew well how to fight, but what chance did we have? Ten against three. And one of us, a baby. William mewled in my arms for his next feed.

'Give me but a little time. I beg you,' John held up his hands. 'I can't pay today. The King's tax has taken my last pennies. Give me until midsummer and I'll find the money. I'll pay you double even.'

'They all say that.' Lancaster's bailiff spat the words. 'Why should we believe you, Ferrour?'

'I'm an honest man. I served your lord in France…'

'Our lord thanks you for your service.' Another man bowed, inciting laughter from his colleagues. They threw open the door and propelled the three of us outside. 'Here is your reward.'

We landed on our backs in the snow. Damp seeped through my kirtle and gripped my limbs like icy fingers. I clutched my shawl and pressed William's shivering body against my shoulder.

'Please sir.' John persisted as his blacksmith tools and the coffer holding our belongings hit the ground. The wooden chest split on impact, scattering my gowns, John's shirts and William's rattle at our feet. 'It's cold. I have a wife and child. And we have nowhere to go.'

I grabbed handfuls of the saturated linen. It would take forever to dry in mid-winter, if it dried at all.

'On your way Ferrour.' The bailiff shrugged. 'Don't be here when we return tomorrow.' He gestured to his men to padlock the door. 'If you are, I won't be able save you from these lads. Merry Christmas.'

We watched shaking as they mounted their horses and rode away.

'Where will we go?' I gripped John's hand as he helped me up to my feet.

'To Rochester.' John picked up his tools and slung them over his back. 'We must pray I can find work there. It's our only hope.'

*

June 1381 – London

A woman's scream echoes down the staircase. Visceral and

raw like when our regiment looted towns and villages in France. My heart pounds. This isn't what we agreed. The traitors we seek are male. Women and children should be left unharmed.

John runs up the steps towards the sound. I unsheathe my blade and follow close behind.

We sprint past the great hall and chapel, and up to the top floor of the keep. The woman shrieks again as we thunder through the King's private apartments, knocking over incense burners and trampling fine carpets.

We enter a bedchamber. The room is twice the size of our Kent smallholding, and dominated by a vast canopied bed. The howling woman cowers on the red and blue silk pillows as our men advance towards her.

She stares over their heads to the door, and our eyes meet. Blue on brown.

Her attackers have torn gems and seed pearls from her cloth of gold gown and veil, exposing her blonde hair and pale skin.

This woman is royal. She has never experienced our suffering and wouldn't understand it. Her lavish clothes and bulging stomach attest to her privileged existence. Her safety isn't my concern. Yet, I can't watch her cornered without feeling sick. Five of our men recline on the bedsheets, their boots staining the royal arms of England with mud. Their companions stand towering over her, daggers and workmen's tools pointing at her neck.

'Come madam.' A red-haired man I don't recognise wriggles nearer to her across the pillows. But I know his type. Opportunists like him skulk after every army, lurking in the shadows for their chance to profit once battle rages. He gropes her breasts with his calloused hands. 'Another kiss. If you wish to live to see your son again.'

'STOP.'

The man's lips are on the woman's, and he is forcing his tongue into her mouth when John shouts.

'Why?' The man snarls, but he pulls back all the same and spins round to glare at John. 'Don't you know who the bitch is? She's no better than a common whore. Why shouldn't I take my turn with her when all the others have?'

'No.' John shoves the man from the bed and onto the floor. The man bangs his head as he falls, and staggers backwards to leave. 'Get out all of you. This isn't what we are here for. We're not savages.' The other men bow their heads and creep away towards the door. 'Remember what the preacher John Ball taught us: "When Adam delved and Eve span, who was the gentleman?" We are all equal before God and worthy of each other's respect, even the King's Mother.'

That's who she is. The legendary Joan of Kent. I shake my head and stare at her, as she glares back. She is often the talk of the Rochester marketplace. I never imagined I would meet her. A woman famed for capturing the heart of a prince with her beauty. Rumoured to have become so rich and haughty since her husband's death that she sleeps surrounded by her jewels. Despicable. Agnes is right. Some souls are beyond salvation.

'Thank you,' she mouths.

We walk away. Neither of us bow or curtsey. King's Mother or no King's Mother. We are building a new world from the ashes of the old. A world where all men and women are equal, and where no child will die of hunger again.

*

'Joanna. Come quick.' Northbourne runs to my side, grinning as we leave the royal apartments. 'Hales and Sudbury are ours. We have them.'

In his armoured breastplate the Kentish knight is a rare creature, a gentleman I trust with my life. He hates Sudbury more than I do, after a land dispute with the Archbishop's men in Canterbury cost him dear. I follow him back down the stairs.

Time slows as I walk. The sounds of struggle, doors being wrenched open, men shouting and objects smashing, fade. I hear only the crunch of my leather soles on the stone steps, and the tap of Northbourne's sheathed sword swaying against his legs.

I blink as Northbourne leads me into St John's chapel. Our men fall silent at my entrance. Afternoon sunlight hits me in the face through the mass of circular windows in the apse like the mailed fist of one of Lancaster's retainers in my face last winter. Golden light floods the chapel and illuminates the space in front of the altar where two men kneel chanting psalms, their eyes fixed on the sparkling crucifix on the altar. Their backs erect as they ignore the fifty men encircling them with pikes and axes. Miserere mei, Deus. Miserere mei.

One man is large with square features and a bald head. His broad body decked out in gold clerical vestments and a purple episcopal cloak. Sudbury. The other is tall and slim. A knight in armour and the red robe of the hospitallers. His crusading order which insists on bleeding England dry to finance their blood lust and hunger for Middle Eastern gold. Hales.

'Take them outside.' My voice echoes through the vast space. I snatch an axe from the hands of the man nearest me, and mime bringing it down through the air. 'And finish them.'

'No.' Sudbury swivels round on his knees, surprisingly agile for an old man. 'We claim the sanctuary of God's house.' He smiles as he brandishes the crucifix on his gold rosary at the men. 'Who among you are willing to risk excommunication and eternal damnation by killing a prince of the church, on the orders of a woman?'

'I am.' Northbourne grips Sudbury under the armpits.

'And me.' The answer rings out from scores of other throats. 'And me.' Sudbury's smile transforms into a grimace as ready hands assist Northbourne and drag him forward across the marble floor. 'Priest or no priest. He must die for his crimes.'

I step aside and let them take Sudbury and Hales

away. They will execute them on Tower Hill as we agreed. Their heads will decorate spikes on London Bridge, and warn others against mistreating common folk.

No need for a trial. Everyone knows Sudbury and Hales are guilty, and the cause of so much suffering for so many. Three poll taxes in four years, and the last the worst of them all. Twelve pence levied on every man and woman whether they were rich or destitute.

I expect to feel joy at justice being served, euphoria even. But I don't. The numbness I've felt since William's death remains. Stubborn and unyielding.

*

December 1380 – Kent

It took us ten days to reach Rochester. Ten days of dragging our feet through snow drifts, while Lancaster and the King celebrated the twelfth night and feasted in the warmth of their halls.

Our stomachs growled unsated by the hunks of stale bread and leftover scraps we begged and foraged on the road.

On the fifth day William went to suckle, and he bit me when no milk came. I had run dry. John and I took turns to press watered-down ale between his lips. But it was no use. Each day his cries grew weaker. By the time Agnes took us into her house in Rochester, and my milk returned, it was too late. He had given up.

He died in my arms the next day. His little face turned away from the breasts of the mother who had failed him.

I clutched tight to his tiny fingers and refused to accept he had closed his brown eyes for the last time.

John fled. We heard him outside chopping wood.

My head spun with questions. What if we had never left France? I should have acted on my misgivings and begged John to let us stay with the army in Gascony. He would have listened; I know he would. Then William would have lived.

For two days I cradled William, singing lullabies and stroking his downy curls. Two days before Agnes and the parish priest lost patience and wrenched his body from me.

I shrieked when they took him.

My son, my precious son was dead. I would never see him again, and it was all my fault.

*

June 1381 – London

A flash of red fabric. Too short to be the outline of a gown, but the right shape for a man's surcoat.

'Wait,' I shout as John goes to leave. Our men have left to dispatch Hales and Sudbury. 'There's someone else up there watching us.' I point up at the musicians' gallery. 'I know there is.'

My heart thunders in my ears and the numbness subsides. I dive for the choir stairs before John can stop me.

John groans. There is a clang which will be him picking up discarded weapons. I don't look back. I no longer care what he is doing.

At the top of the stairs the figure in red comes at me, sword raised. I scream and lift my own knife ready to plunge it into his chest, uncaring if he runs me through in the process. No matter. We will go down together.

'Drop your sword.' John steps between us, axe in hand and the man retreats. As he steps away and his weapon hits the ground, I see he is no man at all. He is a boy, fresh-faced and younger than the King. His brown eyes are soft and wide for all his swagger and pretence at knowing how to fight.

'Who are you?' John snaps.

'Henry of Bolingbroke. Lancaster's son.' The youth smiles and raises himself to his full height, his pride returning. 'I know you hate my father. But I want you to know,

I'm not like the priest Sudbury. I don't fear death. Kill me if you must. I'm ready.'

John roars. He becomes again the man chopping wood in Rochester. The bereaved and helpless father. He raises the axe. Henry shakes his head, and his brown eyes meet mine. Almond eyes.

'NO.' I step between them and knock the axe from John's hand before he can swing and finish Henry. 'I won't kill another mother's son. Let him live for William, and for me.'

Tears well up in my eyes and stream down my cheeks. I'm crying, great desperate sobs. My body shakes as I embrace Henry and he hugs me back.

'You're a good woman,' he says. In my head it is William who speaks not him. You're a good mother. My death was God's will and not your fault. You don't need to fight to find me. I'll be with you always.

'Keep safe,' I whisper. 'Stay hidden until we are gone. Live.'

SHORTLISTED
Muiread O'Hanlon

About the Author

Muiread O'Hanlon is an Irish writer who grew up in Co Down during the Troubles. With a background in human geography and sociology, she has worked in academia for the past twenty-five years researching the lived experience of everyday life. During the pandemic she started to look into her family history which led her to wonder about the lives of her ancestors, particularly those who she knew little about. Following a cancer scare in 2022 she took up creative writing and, inspired by the unknown lives of her ancestors, started to explore the hidden histories of Irish women. She likes to create truths in the gaps in history. In 2023 she was longlisted in the Bedford Writing Competition and in 2024 was shortlisted in the Doris Gooderson Short Story Competition. She has stories published in the New Feathers Anthology and Trasna. Muiread is currently writing her debut novel, Henhouse, the story of a widow who has carried out a horrific deed. The novel explores what is known and unknown and by whom, showing the effects of the values of the nineteen sixties in Ireland (religious, patriarchal, judgemental) on women and children. She loves burrowing down rabbit holes to uncover the context of what she is writing. She has a lot to thank Nelson and Colne College for in helping her find her writing voice and is now an active member of the Writers Ink writing community and the Irish

Writing Centre. She is delighted to have been shortlisted for the Dorothy Dunnett Society / HWA Short Story Award 2024.

Muiread can be contacted at muireadohanlon@gmail.com and followed on Instagram @muireadohanlonauthor and Facebook https://www.facebook.com/muiread.o.hanlon/.

BONFIRE NIGHT
by Muiread O'Hanlon

An armchair appeared overnight, a floral one with holes in it. I am King Billy on his throne, and I gaze up and down the street at my subjects. Jonnie appears dragging an old fridge and I wave him forward.

    Good man. How's about you?

    Grand, he says, smirking at the chair, budge up. No way, I was here first, get your own throne. Jonnie's eleven, six months older than me, and thinks he's a big man. But I got the throne first, so there.

It's a tradition on our street, being King Billy. If there's a chair, whoever gets there first rules for the day. And there's always a chair. This one's pretty knackered but so's my granny's and she'd be raging if I'd took hers, but it must've been somebody's. Before they light the bonfire I'll have to pull it over and add it to the pile which is brill cos I've always wanted to do that. I might let Jonnie help me. I'll have to see.

Have you checked down the back? Jonnie moves with his arm outstretched towards me.

    Away out of it, I say, and kneel in front of the chair.

My fingers reach between the cushion and the left arm of the chair and hoke out wee bits of stuff. Sweet wrappers from a marathon and a mars bar. But also three fluffy love hearts, a black jack, a pencil stub. I wipe the love hearts on my shorts and hand Jonnie the one that says 'forever'.

I rule forever, I say, and he whacks me but takes it anyway and sticks it in his mouth.

Two peelers walk past. Alright boys?

Not getting into any mischief now are you?

We laugh and I offer them the black jack. They grin but say no. I want to ask if they'll show us their guns but that might be pushing my luck. King Billy can only demand so much I suppose, so I go back to rummaging in the armchair.

From the gap beside the right arm I pull out more fluff, two marbles, and a few peanuts. I throw the peanuts into the fire, they're too gone even for me.

I'd of ate those, says Jonnie, and looks at me in disgust. Here, we can play with these, I say, and draw a big circle on the ground with the pencil stub. Jonnie collects some stones and we build an obstacle course and take a marble each. We have to get them through without touching the stones or leaving the circle and it's a right laugh cos we both overshoot and have to go back to the beginning again and again.

You're shite at marbles, says Jonnie, flicking his out of the circle for the umpteenth time.

I s'pose King Billy has other things on his mind today, I say, giving him a punch. It is the eleventh of July after all.

What're you doing now? Jonnie lifts up the cushion that I've thrown onto the road. Shall I stick this on the fire?

Not yet, you eejit, I say, with my arm up to my elbow down the back of the chair. I wave my hand around like a fish swimming in the depths, and pull out a 10p coin. Happy days, I sing, and flick it up in the air. When I catch it I slap it onto the back of my hand, heads or tails, I grin at Jonnie.

Heads, he shouts, the Queen every time.

Like I'd actually give it to him if he called it right. I take my hand away and there's a harp. We stare at it.

It's a harp, I say.

It's a fucken Free State coin, says Jonnie.

I turn it over and a salmon gawps at me. For a moment I consider tossing it into the bonfire with the peanuts. King Billy won't touch fenian coins with a ten foot pole. But then I think, King Billy's no dope. Come on, I say, the McBrides'll take it. We'll get a 10p mix. Grab your Davey to sit in this here chair for me. I'll give him a drum stick for it.

The sweet shop's empty when we get there and Mr McBride doesn't rush us like he does on school days.

Well boys, what are yous up to? Excited for tonight?

I'm King Billy, I tell him. Can I have a 10p mix?

Are you now? Well in that case you'd better have an extra gobstopper, this one has blue and white bubble gum in the middle.

He plops a red ball into the paper bag he's holding and gives me a wink.

When I hand him the coin he shakes his head, all serious. Sure I can't be having that in my shop, he says.

Jonnie and I peer at each other. No smiling now.

Mr McBride looks at me then at Jonnie, opens his mouth and roars with laughter. Sure, I'm only having you on, he says.

We join in and are still laughing when we get back to my throne. Wee Davey is only four but he's held the fort alright.

I sent them packing, he says, and holds out his hand for the drumstick.

I laugh and ruffle his hair. Frig off, he says. He's alright as far as wee brother's go is Davey, in small doses.

We take it in turns to nip home. Bonfire or not, my ma won't have it if we're not back when food's ready.
    No one's going to say I don't feed yous uns, she says, and I won't have you begging round other folks' houses.
    Today it's marmite sandwiches and digestive biscuits. She plonks glasses of milk on the table. I thought about washing my hands like we have to at school but she doesn't remind us so I don't bother. I gulp my food and shoot out the door.
    Be back at five for your tea, she shouts, and I yell, aye ok, as I run off.

Jonnie is sitting on my throne and waves as I kick a stone down the street. The bonfire looks class. More pallets and doors and mattresses have been added and it must be twenty foot high. Older people are hanging around but Jonnie has held his ground and the throne is still mine.

Dare you climb to the top, says Jonnie, and I grin. They've warned us at school about climbing the bonfire, and my ma has said she'd kill me if I tried. Da acted all serious, nodding and agreeing with Ma saying not to, but winking at us behind her back and egging us on. Och it's grand, he said, be a man, it'll be something to tell your grandkids. He'd climbed it at my age, and all my uncles and brothers. It's usually the boys that do it but my oldest sister did it once cos she's a bit of a tomboy. I'd never live it down if I didn't do it too.

The pallets at the bottom are easy enough and I'm eight foot up before I know it.
    I'm the king of the castle, and you're the dirty rascal. I sing at Jonnie and some other kids come to watch me.
    Beyond the pallets there's mattresses and my gutties sink into their softness. Springs poke out in random places

and one sticks into my toe through the hole where the rubber has peeled away from the front of my shoe. My foot is bleeding but I say nothing, King Billy isn't a crybaby. I climb on, use a door handle to lever myself onto an old tyre.

Oi, what you playing at?
 I jump and slip. Shite, it's the McIlroys. They're the ones who light the bonfire, their dad's big in the Orange Order, and Big Mac, the oldest one, plays the Lambeg Drum at the head of the march. All the rest play flutes and pipes. You don't mess with the McIlroys. Last year, when the fire was raging, someone showed up in a balaclava and fired a volley at the picture of the pope. People say was a McIlroy, and I've asked me Da, but if he knows for sure, he won't say. I grab at a table but miss and slip through the tyre into the middle of the bonfire, landing on top of a pallet near the ground again. My head bangs the leg of a chair and I feel a lump come up above my eye.

You ok? Jonnie's voice sounds muffled, scratchy with fear.
 I'm grand, I shout, I coming out now. I figure I can climb back out the way I got in.
 Away and fetch one of them petrol bombs, we'll smoke him out. Big Mac's voice booms inside the bonfire and I freeze.
 Don't do that, begs Jonnie, I swear to God he'll be out soon. Come on, get out of there quick, he shouts to me.
 I start to climb and slip a bit. Jonnie is still begging, please, please he'll be out in a sec, we're only messing. Then silence.
 I climb.
As I emerge at the point I'd fallen in through, Big Mac stands with his hands in his pockets, feet wide apart, staring at me. I say nothing but Jonnie is still whingeing.
 Give over wee lad, he says, stop hopping about, I'm

having you on so I am. And they laugh and knock Jonnie from side to side between them. Big Mac shouts something I don't catch.

What, I shout.

Watch yerself, or you'll end up in the middle again and next time there'll be no mercy, we'll burn you out. He nudges his mate who laughs and draws his finger across his throat.

Go on, he says, see if you're man enough to get to the top.

I climb and climb and a cheer goes up from the small crowd that has gathered to watch. I pose as if I'm sitting on my horse and grin down at Jonnie. It's a wee bit awkward standing there with one foot on a kitchen chair and the other sunk is horsehair oozing from inside a mattress, but I don't let on. The whole town spreads out below me, I'm so high. There's my school and the church. The Presbyterian hall, and the bakery where me ma works while we're at school. And the garage where my da and oldest brother work too. Beyond, there's fields and beyond that the sea. And way beyond there's the mainland. I've never been there but I plan to go when I'm old enough. Everyone says London's a wonderful place.

Here, shouts one of the McIlroys, and pulls something from his pocket, tie this to the top of one of them chairs, and he throws up a ball of green cloth, bound together in a criss-cross of string. When I undo the string and go to drop it into the centre of the bonfire, the big one shouts again, keep the string you buck eejit, you'll need it for the tying. I redden, but they won't see me from there, so I unfurl the ball and watch a tricolour emerge in my hand. A roar comes up from the crowd and I beam as I tie it on.

Jonnie and I take it in turns to go for our tea and at ours tonight it's egg and chips. Mum's always a bit frazzled when she's got the chip pan on and won't stand for any nonsense because once it went on fire and she had to run out the back door and into the yard with it, something she reminds us of every single time. She doesn't even notice my purple, swollen eye which I'm quite proud of now that I've seen it in the mirror.

Don't get under my feet, remember what happened that time?

Yes, we chorus and laugh.

It's no laughing matter she says, I had to throw a wet tea towel over it to put it out.

We know, we shout, still laughing.

And yous aren't ever to make chips yourselves.

We know!

Or play with fire of any kind.

Except the twelfth bonfire, I say, and she throws me a look that says stop it right now.

After tea the crowd has grown and the McIlroys have added my throne to the pile. Wee children are running in circles laughing and pointing at the flag on the top. Down the street, I can still make out where the fire burned through the tarmac last year. The sun lowers in the sky and the street is glorious, the kerbs freshly painted two weeks ago, me and Jonnie working our way up one side and down the other with pots of red, white and blue while the bigger boys hung the bunting and flags between the street lights. It won't get dark until nearly eleven so people start singing and drinking. My ma says I'm too young to drink, and my da says the same, but seeing as I'm ten I figure I'll try some this year if I can fool someone into giving me a swig or two.

The crowd ups a notch and the singing gets louder and the swearing more sweary. Older boys have arrived with their bottles and cigarettes. The mums say, not in front of the weans, but no one hears them. Or cares.

Big Mac, standing beside me now, sets a jerrycan on the ground. Good job, he says, pointing at the flag, it'll burn nicely. There's a gaggle of his followers too and Jonnie and me stand tall, big men with the big men. Where'd you get that coin, he asks, and I go cold.

Coin, I mutter, and he prods me in the shoulder.

Yea, that Free State coin you gave Sammy McBride, are you touts, got some dealings with the Provos?

A chill tingles down my spine and I feel the colour drain from my face.

You bin up the Falls, he says, and I shake my head.

Jonnie remains silent, wide-eyed, trembling.

Big Mac roars and punches me. You should see your faces, he says, I'm having yous on, and he pulls a bottle from his pocket and takes a swig. Here you go wee man, he says, and hands it to me.

I try to laugh but it's a squeak that comes out. Taking the bottle, I spot my mum and dad at the far side of the street and I lift it to my lips, my hands still shaking. I take a gulp. Fuck it burns. I cough and splutter and McIlroy and his gang laugh.

Not so fond of the Bushmills, he says. I'm mortified, but he winks. Jonnie's in creases and so they pass him the bottle. One sip and he's hopping about, clutching his throat, doubled over coughing like crazy. Now everyone's laughing, me too, tears streaming down my face.

Big McIlroy picks up the jerrycan and walks round the bonfire pouring petrol. Someone hands him a lit torch and the two of them walk round the base of the bonfire. Shadows flicker on his face as he thrusts the torch into the bonfire. Sparks fly into the sky as the fire burn. Everyone cheers when the tricolour ignites.

Jonnie can't stand still, he's so excited, and hops up and down, doing a wee dance. That's enough sweeties for you, says his mum, and me and Jonnie laugh. People light sparklers and coloured stars dance from their hands to a chorus of oohs and aahs.

Jonnie paces round the fire, tilting his head, checking it out from all angles. Dare you, I say, and he grins. Jonnie's the best long-jumper in school. Out jumps the older boys, has done for years. One time they took him to Belfast and he came back with a gold trophy which sits on the mantlepiece in his living room, for none of the rest of them ever won a thing.

The embers die down, and everyone's face glows orange. Go on, I whisper to Jonnie, and he backs away to a spot up the hill and runs straight at the fire. His mummy screams noooo as his feet leave the ground and he hovers midair as midnight strikes.

SHORTLISTED
Cath Staincliffe

About the Author

Cath Staincliffe is a best-selling novelist, TV and radio scriptwriter. She is the creator of ITV's hit series, *BLUE MURDER*. Her debut *LOOKING FOR TROUBLE* launched private eye Sal, a single parent juggling work and home, onto Manchester's mean streets. Cath has published a further seven Sal Kilkenny mysteries. Her latest novel, *THE FELLS*, introducing DI Leo Donovan and DC Shan Young has been shortlisted for the People's Book Prize.

Cath's stand-alone novels tell stories of ordinary families caught up in extraordinary events, giving a voice to victims, the bereaved, survivors and witnesses.

THE LOST GIRLS OF ST ANN'S is a move away from crime. A family saga, rooted in Cath's experience as an adoptee growing up in the 1960s, it captures the loss that remains for everyone at the heart of adoption. Cath's own story, of being re-united with her Irish birth family and seven brothers and sisters, featured in the television documentary Finding Cath from RTE.

Cath has been short listed six times for the prestigious CWA Dagger Awards, winning the Short Story Dagger in 2012. *LETTERS TO MY DAUGHTER'S KILLER* was selected for Specsavers Crime Thriller Book Club in 2014 and featured on ITV3's Crime Thriller Club. Cath was a joint winner of the WGGB Best Radio Drama Award 2019 for STONE S7. *RUNNING OUT OF ROAD* was short-listed for the eDunnit best novel Award at CrimeFest 2022.

Cath is a founder member of *Murder Squad*, a virtual collective of northern crime writers.

www.cathstaincliffe.co.uk
@CathStaincliffe (X)
@cathstaincliffe.bsky.social

NEBRASKA
by Cath Staincliffe

Britta had a notion she could smell smoke. She opened the cabin door and stood on the threshold, chin raised, nostrils flaring, ears pricked.

Their own fire, in the pit close by, was out for the night. The smoke from their nearest neighbours, squatters way down the mountain, rarely reached so far.

She closed her eyes, the better to listen for foreign sounds among the whistle of crickets and the rustle of mice and rats and voles.

Stepping outside, Britta rooted her bare feet wide in the dusty grit, feeling for vibrations.

Was it them fellas from last year?

Were they coming back?

Or others like them?

Poised to act, to rouse her brothers and flee as they had practised, she bade herself wait. She endured the savage attention of mosquitoes and the prickle of sweat across her neck. She sipped at the air but could no longer discern the burning scent.

A screech from the ravine, the clatter of claws and the beating of wings, startled her and broke the spell.

Inside she lay down beside the boys in the dark, her heart still thumping.

Not tonight, she told herself.

Maybe never, she prayed.

They came five weeks later. In daylight. Britta was on her way to fetch water from the creek when she felt the shudder underfoot, the percussion of hooves.

She flew back up the hill and whistled to the boys. Their special sign, like the sweet song of the mountain bluebird.

Erik, the youngest, darted from behind the cabin. He stopped when he saw her, mouth opening, a plea she surmised to fetch some keepsake from the house, his toy tin horse in all likelihood. She shook her head and on they ran, fleet as jackrabbits, melting through the sage-scrub like ice-water in spring. The older boy, Lars, was down the hole already when they arrived.

'You see them?' He panted as he reached up to help the little one down the last stretch.

'No,' she said.

The chimney-like entrance twisted near the bottom so the cave itself was concealed from view, should a body have the inclination to wander around the cliffs searching.

She imagined the men ransacking the cabin, arguing about the pitiful plunder. Not a darn thing worth taking.

Imagined they had caught her.

'Leastaways there is this little cat.'

'Bring her with us. Break her in and sell her on.'

'You going to be a good puss now?' Leering at her. Pawing. A fourteen-year-old virgin.

'How long?' Erik asked.

'Morning at least.' They would be gone by morning, she hoped.

Gone one way or another.

Their hidey hole was cramped, they sat knees almost touching. The silted floor was hard and smelled sour. Scant light penetrated the shaft.

They passed the time whispering stories, taking sips of water from the canteen that it was Erik's job to maintain. Pulling it up on its twine and refilling it twice a week in preparation for such a time as this.

Was it the same men? Was that of concern?

The light faded and the rock about them creaked and clicked in the cooling air. In full dark Britta prised open the tin she had filled with nuts and stored here and they shared them, cracking the wrinkled shells between their teeth to winkle out the meat.

Lars wanted to pee and they agreed to shuffle even closer together to allow one side of the cave for a toilet. He could not get going at first, and that made them all laugh, and then Erik complained about the stink.

'Sleep now.' Britta told them. Erik nestled into her lap in the night. His head a heavy ball on her stomach, making her shift damp. His knees bony against her hip.

He smelled bitter. These past months his gums had bled and patches, rough like buckeye bark, flared on his skin. There was never enough to eat.

Mamma had grown beans and herbs in the thin soil and instructed them which plants they could forage for and which were poisonous. Pappa had traded his moonshine, and sometimes his labour, for other supplies. Britta used to help him brew, mixing the sugar and water, heating then cooling the copper pot. With them both gone life was a hard row.

'Run!' her mamma had screamed, her voice raw with terror. The children had bolted. The crack of a gunshot rent the air, the sound a blow to Britta's spine making her stagger. The three of them had hidden in a shallow gully until thirst, and dread, forced them home. Erik delirious with fever.

Pappa was dead, shot in the chest, fallen outside the

cabin. Mamma was taken along with the good plate and their tools and the Swedish blanket. And most of Pappa's rotgut.

They could not bury him. The rock was unforgiving. Instead Britta and Lars had dragged him from the cabin, a way away, and gathered stones to cover him. But there were precious few and the rats and crows and flies kept pestering. So Britta had hauled out their parents straw pallet and they rolled Pappa's body onto it and covered him with branches of sage and she had poured liquor over him and set it alight. Erik had screamed but Britta had calmed him, talking of other lands, other times, where this was done. The Hindus of the Indian subcontinent, the Norsemen and their longships. Their very own ancestors. Seafarers.

They had never seen the sea.

The smell of that smoke haunted her dreams.

'What if they come back?' Erik had said.

'We will make a plan to hide somewhere they'll never find us,' Britta said.

She didn't want to hide. She wanted to ambush them. Shoot them full of lead, cut their throats, break their necks. Hang them. Flay them. Kill them stone dead.

'It's morning.' Lars yawned.

'Stay here,' Britta said. She scaled the shaft and emerged blinking against the sun which glanced white off the rock. She heard a horse whinny. They were still here.

The day passed. A second night. They were famished. Stiff. Peevish.

Britta barely slept, twitching at every rustle and squeak, her skin tight, insides knotted. How long must they wait? How long was enough?

At sunrise they climbed out and filed quietly down the cliff towards the cabin.

Britta tested the air, no scent of smoke.

A ripple of movement on the ground. A copperhead!

She stopped rigid, arm raised to warn the boys. The snake slithered past, all chestnut and orange patterns, and into the scrub.

Britta heard the horse whinny again.

Inching forward she came to the cabin from the west where the light was dimmer.

The horses, two of them, a bay and a pinto, were tied to the old rail her pappa had fashioned more in hope than expectation.

One whickered at her approach. The other shifted, a sidestep in the dust.

Britta froze. Listened.

The door to the cabin was closed.

She crept closer, her tongue clamped between her teeth, the pulse in her temple thudding. Edging to the door until she could lift the latch.

The bodies lay curled where they had fallen. The stench of vomit and befoulment was overpowering. That and the sickly fruit smell of the moonshine. Both bottles were half empty, abandoned between the two men. This batch she had brewed herself, carefully adding hemlock from the plants down by the creek. Then leaving the vintage in plain sight for the taking. Knowing they were likely partial to a drop.

The family's meagre possessions were strewn about, baskets and the T-chest turfed out. She thought of them rifling through their worldly goods, disparaging, avaricious.

Covering her nose and mouth she moved closer and peered at them. Her eyes locked upon the ring. Her pappa's signet ring on a dead man's hand.

Britta whistled for her brothers. Stepping carefully she picked up the men's saddlebags, and the gun belts on the makeshift table. And Erik's toy from where it lay.

'Did it work?' Lars called.

'It worked.'

She came outside, arms laden.

'Check these bags for food. We should eat first,'

she said.

'First? And then what?' Erik asked, reaching out for his toy horse.

She smiled and nodded to the animals. 'We are going on a ride.'

His face glowed. 'Where?'

'Away,' she said. 'Someplace new.' They could sell one of the guns, and anything of value in the bags, trade one of the horses, and find a place to settle.

Lars met her eyes, nodded.

'But Mamma?' Erik said.

'Mamma will understand.'

Britta was smiling but her eyes burned. Probably just the sun so bright already. She slapped her thighs and cleared her throat and went to water the horses.

Many thanks to our first-round judges:
Karen Alvey
Jean Lang
Betty Moxon
Kate Jewell
Barbara Milner
Ned Palmer
Ellen Rawson
Imogen Robertson

And our final-round judges:
Janet Angelini
Katherine Clements
Norah Perkins
Flora Rees

Many congratulations to all the longlisted writers:
Friends - Erika Banerji
Forgotten - Mary Byrne
The Silence of the Gulls - Anne Byrne
Purity - Joseph Dragovich
The Starlings' Call - Emma Fielder
Those Unheard - Nanci Gilliver
The King's Question - Clare Hawkins
Mother and Mary - Colette Lawlor
Sentry Duty - M.E. Lawrence
The Pioneer Spirit - Colleen MacMahon
The Archbishop's Confession - Alice McVeigh
Lunardi's Ascent - Tony Oswick
The Skull of Lady Alice FitzJohn - Jack Sanger
Hands - Amber Sayer
It All Depends on Portland - Markene Shinn Lewis
Canaries - Martin Tulton
Venus with Pistachios - Josie Turner
Sugar Moon - B.J. Weary

The Promised Land - Emily Zinkin

About the Dorothy Dunnett Society

Dorothy Dunnett relished her relationship with her readers, listening to their views and always replying to their letters. She set up the Dorothy Dunnett Society to help us to keep in touch with each other and to promote discussion and debate about history, literature and art, as well as her ever-fascinating characters, and in so doing helped create an international community of readers.

The Society has over 750 members around the world who receive *Whispering Gallery*, our quarterly magazine about all things Dunnett with articles about characters and sources, as well as the history and art of the times in which the books are set, together with fascinating extracts from Dorothy Dunnett's archive. The Society is also active on social media (Fb, X and Instagram)

Dunnett readers around the world love nothing more than getting together to share their common interests in history, art, music and books. There is an annual Dunnett Weekend in Scotland and local gatherings in different places around the world. There have been organised journeys to favourite Dunnett locations such as Malta, Venice and Istanbul and many individual and small group excursions. Each year we celebrate International Dorothy Dunnett Day on the second Saturday in November, when members all around the world meet in groups large and small with a celebratory glass raised at 1pm (local time).

2023 was a special year for the Society as it marked the centenary of Dorothy Dunnett's birth. Over 270 delegates met in Edinburgh to attend Centenary celebrations, with a 2-day academic conference on the theme of Understanding Diversity in the 15th and 16th Centuries, our annual conference, and many trips, events, and meals, together with a glorious concert of renaissance music in St Giles. The Society also created a special Centenary website Dorothy Dunnett Centenary (dunnettcentral.org) where you can read more about Dorothy Dunnett's life and work.

An innovation for 2024 is DunNET – a series of international on-line lectures on topics of interest to readers – the first in September was Dr Jennifer L Wood talking about "Musical diplomacy on the global stage: Dallam's organ and Lymond's spinet".

The Society also has its own shop where you can buy all sorts of things, from mugs to the Dorothy Dunnett Guides to important locations: Istanbul, Bruges, Orkney and North-East Scotland, Iceland, Russia and Edinburgh are available in the shop on the Dorothy Dunnett Society website (and more are in the pipeline): https://dunnettcentral.org.

Many of Dorothy Dunnett's books are available as audiobooks on audible – long and immersive reads.

In addition to her major historical novels *The Lymond Chronicles* and *The House of Niccolo*, Dorothy Dunnett wrote lighter thrillers, originally published under her maiden name of Dorothy Halliday. They are now available from Farrago Press (and on kindle) with splendidly stylish covers. They feature Johnson Johnson, an enigmatic portrait painter with a yacht called Dolly and a variety of Dunnett's splendid female characters as well as exotic locations, derring do and humour. The titles (in the suggested order of reading) are: *Tropical Issue* (*Dolly and the Bird of Paradise*) 1983; *Rum Affair* (*Dolly and the Singing Bird; The Photogenic Soprano*) 1968; *Ibiza Surprise* (*Dolly and the Cookie Bird; Murder in the Round*) 1970; *Operation Nassau* (*Dolly and the Doctor Bird; Match for a Murderer*) 1971; *Roman Nights* (*Dolly and the Starry Bird; Murder in Focus*) 1973; *Split Code* (*Dolly and the Nanny Bird*) 1976;

About the Historical Writers' Association

Our passion is history. We are authors, publishers, bloggers and agents of historical writing, both fiction and non-fiction, and we created the HWA to promote, support and connect our members, and to introduce readers to brilliant books. Whatever type of historical writing you are looking for you'll find HWA members are writing it. Wartime adventures, court intrigues, extraordinary explorations of ordinary lives, the swirl of social change and new perspectives on every aspect of our past, all bound up by superb story-telling. Our growing social media following allows readers and writers to connect and share their enthusiasms and interests as well as letting book buyers into the secret histories which lie behind every line our members write.

Historia is our online magazine for readers of historical fiction and non-fiction. Updated every week with reviews, feature articles, writing advice and interviews it has a dedicated audience and a growing list of subscribers. Regular giveaways, behind the scenes insights into the writing life and a fresh, modern voice make it the place to discover your new favourite author, find the next novel for your book group or find in-depth discussions of how and why we write what we do.

www.historiamag.com
www.historicalwriters.org

Printed in Great Britain
by Amazon